101 WAYS
TO SET YOUR
SOUL ON FIRE

MESSAGES FROM A MEDIUM
TO IGNITE YOUR SOUL PURPOSE

MICHELLE CLARE

ISBN: 979-8-9989292-0-5

DEDICATION

For my Dad, Ashley, Sophie, and Josh

You are the heartbeat of my journey, the soul of my becoming, and the sacred home of my heart.

Dad, your quiet strength and unwavering love have been the ground beneath me - the silent, steady force guiding every step I've taken.

Ashley, Sophie, and Josh - your love is the divine grace that walks beside me across lifetimes. You are my miracles, my reminders that love is eternal, unshakable, and true.

Your souls have danced with mine through realms seen and unseen, reminding me that those destined to walk with us will always return - across time, space, and story.

This book is born of divine purpose, wrapped in deep gratitude, and offered as a sacred piece of my spirit - a vessel of love, memory, and truth that reaches far beyond this lifetime.

May you always remember the luminous, powerful souls that you are.

INSPIRED BY

With deep gratitude to Jeff Janssen…

Your light, wisdom, and unwavering support helped inspire this book. Your guidance awakens purpose in others, and your heartfelt work reminds us all why we are here.

CONTENTS

Introduction   i

1 Joy   1
2 What Would You Like?   2
3 Take The Step   3
4 Life, It Is a Never-ending Story   4
5 Have Faith, There Is Divine Timing   5
6 Will I Miss What Is Meant for Me?   6
7 What Does "Heaven" Feel Like?   7
8 Nothing Is Impossible   8
9 You Are Present on Earth at This Specific Time for a Reason   9
10 Life Is Short. Enjoy The Journey   10
11 Don't Be Afraid of Your Own Shadow, We All Have One   11
12 Be Present   12
13 A Missed Opportunity or A Blessing in Disguise?   13
14 Before You Set Your Goals, Focus on Your "Why" To Move Forward   15
15 Know Your Powers   16
16 It's A New Cycle, Now What?   17
17 Letting Go of the Old and Bringing in the New   19
18 Decide Your Life Is Magical   21
19 Stand In the Power of Your Soul   22
20 We Connect to Spirit in The Subtle Whispers of Life   23
21 Trust Yourself Enough to Take the Next Step   24
22 Don't Look Back   26
23 You Owe It to Yourself to Become Everything You Dream of Becoming   27
24 In The Story of Your Life, You Are the Hero   28

25   This Is Just a Season, Stay Present. There Are   29
Lessons to Be Learned and Room to Grow

26   Seeing With Fresh Eyes Leads to   30
Transformations

27   Transformation Begins with The Acceptance   31
of What Is

28   Dear Humans, You Are Love   32

29   Blending The Human Soul into The Eternal   33
Spirit

30   It's Always Darkest Before the Light, Keep   34
Going!

31   On A Soul Level, Every Moment of Your Life   35
Matters

32   Memories Of Heaven, The Light Came from   36
Within

33   This Life Is the Dream   37

34   Light Workers, You Are Being Called into   38
Action Now

35   Just For Today   39

36   The Gift of Time   40

37   Love Is Not a Place or a Person, It's an   41
Energy

38   The Hardest Part Is Letting Go   42

39   We Don't Break Open So That the Light Can   43
Get In, We Break Open So That the World
Can See Our Inner Light

40   Finding Your Soul's True North   44

41   As The Fog Lifts   45

42   Every Prayer We Pray Has Been Prayed   46
Before

43   The Journey of Becoming   47

44   Never Alone   48

45   Mediumship Helpful Tips   49

46   When You Are in the Flow with Life   50
Things Happen Effortlessly

47   Trust The Process of Your Divine Path   51

48   Intuition, The Whisper That Turns into a   52
Roar

49	We Open Like a Rose	53
50	Your Loved Ones on The Other Side Are Watching Over You	54
51	Dig Deeper, You've Got This!	55
52	Your Deepest Pain Can Launch You on The Path to Your Greatest Calling	56
53	There Is a Calmness That Comes When We Realize It's Time to Move Forward	57
54	The Storm	58
55	Passing By Suicide	59
56	You Can Make the World a Little Brighter and Kinder	60
57	Refuse To Settle	61
58	With Every Goodbye, We Learn	62
59	You've Got This!	63
60	Being The Light	64
61	What Do You Really Want?	65
62	If You Focus on the Lessons, You Will Find Your Way	66
63	Trust In the Magic of The Universe	67
64	Stand In Your Power, Beautiful Soul	68
65	Believe In Yourself	69
66	Raise Your Standards	70
67	Make A Wish	71
68	The Bridge Will Appear	72
69	Your Purpose Is to Fully Be Who You Are	73
70	Discovering What Makes You Truly Happy	74
71	It's Time to Thrive	75
72	Dream Bigger	76
73	Who Am I Now?	77
74	Be The Best Version of Yourself and Know That You Are Needed in This World	78
75	Everyone Has a Guardian Angel	79
76	Embrace This Moment	80
77	Give Yourself Permission to Simply Be	81
78	Love Lives On	82

79	Invest In Yourself	83
80	Synchronicity	84
81	Starting Over	85
82	Make Peace with Yourself	86
83	Make The World a Better, Brighter Place	87
84	Celebrating The Divine Mother	88
85	Heal Yourself	89
86	Be Here Now	90
87	In The Quiet Moments, You Can Hear God Speak	91
88	Loved Ones in Spirit	92
89	Find The Magic in Life	93
90	Choose Peace Within	94
91	A Season of Endings	95
92	What If, Just for Today, You Surrender to the Conflict, Pain, And Chaos in Your Life?	96
93	You Are a Soul	97
94	The Ocean of Life	98
95	Celebrating The Divine Father	99
96	The Time Is Now	100
97	Even In the Wake of Tragedy, Life Holds the Promise of Beauty Once More	101
98	Be Patient with Yourself	102
99	Life	103
100	You Are Made to Exist In The Frequency of Love	104
101	Your Soul Is Saying to You	105
	About the Author	106

INTRODUCTION

Your soul didn't come here to play small. It came to awaken, to rise, to remember its brilliance and set the world alight with truth, purpose, and passion. You are not here by accident. Your soul chose this life, this moment, this very breath — to remember who you truly are. This book is a call to that remembering.

101 Ways to Set Your Soul on Fire is more than a book; it's a cosmic whisper, a sacred ignition, a guide back to the brilliance already within you.

Within these pages are sparks—sacred reminders, bold invitations, and soul-stirring truths—meant to awaken the embers of your spirit, to stir the ancient knowing that still lives in your bones, igniting the fire within you.

Whether you're standing at the edge of transformation, lost in the in-between, or ready to leap into your highest calling, these 101 messages are here to guide you home to yourself. Unlock deeper truths. Ignite dormant dreams and align with your soul's highest path.

May each word fan the flames of your divine light. May you burn away the doubt, rise from the ashes, and live as the radiant soul you were always meant to be. May this journey reawaken the fire you've always carried. And may you remember, with every page, that you are divine, limitless, and already whole.

The light is in you. Let it rise.

Dear Michelle,

What a journey you have planned for yourself! It is ambitious; you have big hopes and big dreams. You will also have many challenges and heartbreaks to overcome. You will have three Near Death Experiences, and each one will change, create, and grow not only your humanness but, most importantly, the fabric of your soul.

In your third Near Death Experience, you will be given the choice to stay on earth or to come home to this realm that is called Heaven. You will begin to refer to this as the most pivotal moment of your life - when time stood still. In that moment, surrounded by angels, life guides, and unconditional love, you will see your beautiful children and decide to stay on earth longer. This choice comes with a mission and more challenges. You will agree to follow your passion of being a medium, but your twenty-five year marriage will end in divorce. You will fall in love again, and he will die by suicide. It will feel like the year 2023 is trying to break you, and you will be on your knees.

But wait, there is so much more…

Michelle, in those moments during your life where you feel like you cannot take the next breath or the next step, help will miraculously show up. You will be surrounded by the kindest, wisest, most loving people - old friends, new friends, and strangers. They will show you true pure love, strength, courage, and most importantly, remind you of who you are. You will have friends that wipe your tears, carry you to your next step, and cheer you on. You will choose to find gratitude instead of bitterness & resentment, and you will be able to see all of the love that exists in this world and still live life with an open heart. What a gift! After all, you came here to experience earthly life and love, and you will do both.

Don't ever forget that you will never be alone on this journey. God, the angels, your life guides, and loved ones in Spirit are walking with you every step of the way. Until it is your turn to go home again, you will find amazing, loving, and kind humans every day. This life is a blessing, and it is meant to be lived. Keep breathing, keep smiling, and keep loving.

Forever Grateful,
Michelle

1

Joy

Whatever you do next, do it for the joy it brings you. Let your actions be guided by passion and enthusiasm, allowing the pursuit of happiness to be your compass. Engage in activities that light up your soul, filling your heart with excitement and fulfillment. Whether it's a small, everyday task or a grand, ambitious project, infuse it with your unique energy and zest for life. By prioritizing joy in your endeavors, you not only enrich your own experience but also inspire those around you. Embrace the journey with a spirit of adventure and delight, knowing that true success lies in the happiness and satisfaction that come from doing what you love.

2

What Would You Like?

One of the most mind-expanding questions…
Is one that requires you to set aside all your fears and
doubts… and to simply dream.

"What would you attempt if you knew you could not
fail?"

It embeds one of life's most important
questions, "What would you like?"

It is through our wants and desires that we reach out to
life.

And when we reach out to life, life expands.

So, "What would you like?" If you knew you could not
fail.

3

Take The Step

New beginnings tend to start because of an ending. It is okay to not feel ready; it is okay to feel unsteady. But take this opportunity to create the life that you want to live. Embracing new beginnings requires courage, resilience, and an open heart, inviting us to step forward into the unknown with optimism and a sense of possibility. You are so strong and loved beyond measure.

Take the step, brave soul.

4

Life, It Is a Never-ending Story

Life is a journey of profound significance, where each step, each encounter, carries a deeper purpose, guiding the soul toward growth and enlightenment. Every moment, whether bathed in joy or shrouded in challenges, holds a sacred resonance, offering opportunities for self-discovery and spiritual evolution. The trials faced and triumphs celebrated are threads intricately sewn into the fabric of existence, enriching the soul's narrative and expanding its wisdom.

Within this sacred journey, the soul finds resonance in the whispers of nature, the symphony of human connections, and the quietude of introspection. It navigates through seasons of change, embracing the ebb and flow of life's rhythm, understanding that within every experience lies a hidden gem, a lesson waiting to be unraveled. The journey isn't merely a passage from earthly birth to earthly death; it's a profound voyage where the soul seeks understanding, compassion, and an unshakeable connection to the universe, finding its place amidst the grandeur of existence for eternity. Take time to marvel at your journey.

5

*H*ave Faith
There Is Divine Timing

In the serene embrace of faith, I entrust my desires to the flow of divine timing. Like a gentle current guiding a river to its destination, I surrender to the wisdom of the universe. I believe that every dream, every aspiration, is intricately woven into the fabric of existence, awaiting its perfect moment to arrive. With patience as my ally and trust as my compass, I navigate the twists and turns of life's journey, knowing that each step brings me closer to the fruition of my dreams. In the tapestry of time, every thread is purposeful, every delay a blessing in disguise. With unwavering faith, I embrace the unfolding of my destiny, knowing that in the fullness of time, all that is meant for me will gracefully manifest.

6

Will I Miss What Is Meant for Me?

If something is meant for you, the universe will ensure its arrival holds a captivating allure. There is a profound intertwining of destiny and cosmic alignment, implying that certain paths, connections, or opportunities are destined to find their way to you. This embodies faith in the unseen forces orchestrating the flow of life, reassuring individuals that what's truly meant to be theirs will manifest.

This also reminds us about the essence of patience, trust, and surrender, fostering a sense of calm amidst uncertainty, affirming that The Universe operates in mysterious yet purposeful ways, ultimately guiding each individual toward their next endeavor. Rest assured, what is meant for you will find you. Have faith in your faith, my friends. The Universe has unlimited gifts available for you.

7

What Does "Heaven" Feel Like?

After three Near Death Experiences (or as some call them-Nearer to Life Experiences) I can give you a glimpse.

Start by imagining: a radiant light that encompasses you with unfaltering love and permeates you with an abundance of peace.

Heaven feels like a boundless embrace of serenity, love and bliss. It's a realm where tranquility and joy intermingle effortlessly, where the essence of peace permeates everything. Imagine the purest form of contentment, an overwhelming sense of fulfillment that transcends time and space. It's an endless symphony of harmony, where hearts are weightless and spirits soar in eternal happiness. In heaven, there's an indescribable warmth, an embrace of love that envelops every soul, creating a haven where every moment is infused with profound and unending joy.

You are still connected to all of your loved ones on the Earth in an endless bond that cannot be broken.

8

Nothing Is Impossible

There is a place inside of you where nothing is impossible.

Deep within the recesses of the human soul lies a sacred realm where the boundaries of possibility dissolve into the infinite. It's a place untouched by the constraints of the physical world, where imagination dances freely and dreams take shape without inhibition. Here, the whispers of aspirations echo endlessly, nurturing the seeds of potential into magnificent realities. In this inner sanctum, the heart's desires intertwine with the power of belief, birthing a universe where limits cease to exist. It's a canvas waiting to be painted with the vibrant hues of hope, resilience, and unwavering faith—a sanctuary where the impossible finds its footing and transforms into the possible.

Within this sacred space of the soul, one discovers an eternal wellspring of courage and resilience, where the human spirit reigns supreme, fostering an unwavering belief that indeed, nothing is impossible.

9

*Y*ou Are Present on Earth
At This Specific Time for a Reason

Each individual gracing this earth at this precise
moment embodies a purpose intricately woven into the
fabric of existence. It's a convergence of souls across
time and space, each bearing unique gifts, perspectives,
and contributions crucial to the unfolding narrative of
humanity. Whether as catalysts of change, stewards of
wisdom, champions of compassion, or architects of
innovation, every person incarnated in this era carries a
distinct role within the collective evolution of our
world.

Consciously or intuitively, individuals navigate the
currents of change, contributing to the collective
consciousness through innovation, advocacy, or
compassionate endeavors. The interconnectedness of
life and the interplay of diverse perspectives underscore
the significance of each being's role, reinforcing the
belief that their presence in this precise moment is no
random occurrence but a purposeful plan in the grand
narrative of human evolution.

10

Life Is Short. Enjoy The Journey

Life is short, and this is your reminder to savor each fleeting moment, to immerse ourselves wholly in the present and relish the beauty of the journey. Amidst the hustle and bustle, it's easy to get entangled in the webs of tomorrow's uncertainties or yesterday's reminisces. Yet, within the grasp of our hands lies the gift of today—a canvas waiting for us to paint it with vibrant experiences, cherished connections, and moments that resonate deep within our souls. Life's true essence unfolds in the richness of these present moments, in the laughter shared, in the serene pauses, and in the simple joys that color our days. It urges us not to merely exist but to thrive in the beauty of each passing moment, embracing the ebbs and flows with open arms, knowing that within them lie lessons, growth, and precious memories.

11

Don't Be Afraid of Your Own Shadow
We All Have One

The shadow side, often shrouded in mystery and misunderstood, harbors facets of ourselves we tend to shun or fear. Yet, delving into this unexplored terrain unveils profound opportunities for growth and self-understanding. Embracing our shadow side means acknowledging the complexities within, accepting the parts that lie in the shadows, waiting to be illuminated. It's a courageous journey of self-discovery, where we confront our vulnerabilities, fears, and insecurities, realizing that these aspects are integral to our holistic existence. By embracing our shadows, we unlock the potential for profound transformation, gaining insights that enable us to navigate life with newfound wisdom and compassion.

The shadow side isn't a realm to be feared, but rather a mirror reflecting the entirety of our being. It's within this darkness that we find the seeds of resilience and strength, waiting to be unearthed. After all, shadows have nowhere to go when you bring in the light.

12

*B*e *Present*

To be present is to embark on an inner pilgrimage, acknowledging the marvels of existence and being attuned to the whispers of the here and now. It's about anchoring ourselves in the present, allowing ourselves to be fully immersed in the experience unfolding before us, unburdened by the weight of what's to come or what has passed. The journey of life unfolds in the intricacies of everyday living, and within it resides a treasure trove of opportunities for self-discovery, learning, and profound connections with others.

Embracing the present grants us the gift of mindfulness, a conscious embrace of the present moment, fostering a deeper appreciation for the beauty woven into the fabric of our lives. As we cherish each moment, we weave a tapestry of memories, love, and experiences that enrich the tapestry of our existence.

13

A Missed Opportunity Or A Blessing in Disguise?

Missed opportunities often carry a veil of disappointment, masking the hidden blessings they may conceal. These moments, seemingly lost in time, often redirect our course toward unforeseen paths brimming with new possibilities. They serve as poignant reminders that what we perceive as a setback, actually might be for our highest good. Sometimes, the roads not taken lead us toward unexpected experiences, allowing room for personal growth and the cultivation of new dreams. In hindsight, these missed chances act as guiding lights, nudging us toward more fitting opportunities that align better with our aspirations and personal development.

Moreover, these apparent missteps often foster a deeper appreciation for the journey itself. They encourage introspection and reflection, imparting invaluable lessons that might have been overlooked in the rush toward immediate success. Missed opportunities can provide the space needed to recalibrate our ambitions, sometimes leading to discoveries of untapped potential or avenues that better resonate with our passions and values. In essence, these overlooked moments can paradoxically unfold into unforeseen blessings, guiding us toward richer experiences and a more fulfilling life. Don't forget to count your blessings.

14

Before You Set Your Goals, Focus On Your "Why" To Move Forward

This guiding light serves as a compass, steering you through the tumultuous seas of uncertainty, grounding your decisions in a bedrock of meaning and significance. Understanding your "why" breathes life into aspirations, transforming mere goals into impassioned missions. It imbues your actions with clarity, aligning your efforts with a greater sense of purpose that transcends mere accomplishments and delves into the realm of impact and fulfillment.

Your "why" serves as a constant reminder of the reasons propelling you forward. It's the anchor amidst the tempest, grounding you in moments of doubt or distraction. By honing in on your "why," you forge a profound connection between your actions and their underlying significance, fostering resilience in the face of adversity and infusing your journey with a sense of direction. This focus channels your energy towards endeavors that resonate with your core values, ultimately leading to a more purposeful, meaningful, and gratifying path in life.

15

Know Your Powers

Know your powers, for they are the essence of your influence and the keys to unlocking your potential. Your words hold the power to uplift, inspire, and create change; choose them wisely and speak with intention. Your silence, too, is powerful, offering space for reflection, understanding, and the quiet strength of presence. Your mind is a vast reservoir of creativity and wisdom; nurture it, challenge it, and let it guide you towards your dreams. Your body language communicates volumes, often more than words can express; use it to convey confidence, empathy, and authenticity. Lastly, your energy is a force that resonates with others, shaping the atmosphere around you; cultivate positivity, passion, and purpose. Embrace and harness these powers, for they define your impact and illuminate your path.

16

*I*t's *A New Cycle, Now What?*

Shaping a transformative shift in life begins with embracing the power of presence and gratitude. Being present means immersing oneself fully in the current moment, freeing the mind from the shackles of the past and the uncertainties of the future. It involves fostering awareness of the beauty, lessons, and opportunities inherent in the present circumstances. When we are truly present, we engage more deeply with experiences, relationships, and surroundings, thereby opening ourselves to newfound perspectives and pathways for growth. Coupled with this presence is the practice of gratitude—a profound acknowledgment of the blessings, big and small, that enrich our lives. A heart filled with gratitude serves as a catalyst for change, amplifying positivity, resilience, and a deep sense of contentment amidst life's ebb and flow.

Choosing to live with a heart full of gratitude fuels a transformational journey toward a more fulfilling life. It's about recognizing and appreciating the abundance that surrounds us, whether in moments of joy or amidst challenges. Gratitude allows us to navigate life's complexities with grace, fostering a mindset that focuses on what we have rather than dwelling on what's lacking.

This shift in perspective not only cultivates inner peace but also attracts positivity, abundance, and opportunities into our lives. Being present and embracing gratitude become intertwined forces, guiding us toward personal evolution, fostering resilience, and paving the way for the profound changes we seek in our lives. Let's start now with the gentle thought of 'just for today.' Remember: life can only be lived one second, one minute, one hour, one day at a time.

17

Letting Go of the Old And Bringing In the New

Letting go of the old signifies a courageous embrace of growth and renewal. It's a tender act of bidding adieu to chapters that have served their purpose, releasing the weight of past narratives that might no longer align with our evolving selves. There's a poignant beauty in acknowledging that the past, while a cherished teacher, need not define the entirety of our journey. It's about honoring the lessons gleaned, the joys shared, and the hardships endured, yet summoning the courage to loosen our grip on what no longer serves our higher purpose. This act of release is fostering space for fresh experiences, new connections, and uncharted pathways to unfold.

Bringing in the new unfolds like a blank canvas awaiting the strokes of a masterpiece. It's an invitation to welcome unexplored possibilities and embrace the thrill of uncertainty. This transition isn't solely about turning a new page; it's about seizing the opportunity to script a narrative infused with intention and authenticity. As we step into this unknown territory, we carry with us the resilience forged by past experiences and the wisdom cultivated through trials. It's a chance to redefine ourselves, to embody the aspirations that whisper in the depths of our hearts. Embracing the new isn't just a momentary change; it's an ongoing journey of self-discovery, resilience, and the continual pursuit of a more enriched and fulfilling existence.

18

Decide Your Life Is Magical

The day you decide your life is magical marks a significant shift in perspective and perception. It's a choice to view the world through a lens that amplifies the beauty, wonder, and possibility inherent in every moment. This decision isn't about an immediate transformation of circumstances but rather a profound shift in attitude—a commitment to seeking and recognizing the extraordinary in the ordinary.

From that day forward, you begin to notice the intricate patterns woven into the fabric of existence. The sunrise becomes a symphony of colors, laughter echoes like music, and each interaction brims with the potential for connection and growth. This shift in perception doesn't erase challenges or difficulties, but it alters the way you navigate them. It infuses resilience, hope, and an unyielding belief in the magic that resides within and around you. It's a conscious choice to live with an open heart and a heightened awareness, embracing life as an ever-unfolding tale of enchantment waiting to be explored.

19

Stand In the Power of Your Soul

Standing in the power of your soul is akin to unfurling the wings of your spirit, ready to take flight into the vast expanse of possibilities. It's an alignment with the deepest essence of your being, a resonant harmony between your inner truth and the external world. When you embrace this power, your soul becomes a beacon guiding you towards authenticity, purpose, and boundless potential. It's a profound realization that within you resides an unyielding strength, a wisdom untethered by constraints, urging you to soar beyond limitations and embrace the limitless horizons of your existence. Standing in the power of your soul, you are not just a spectator but an active participant in the symphony of life, ready to spread your wings and take flight into the realms of fulfillment, creativity, and profound self-discovery.

20

We Connect to Spirit
In The Subtle Whispers of Life

Connecting to Spirit often involves attuning oneself to the delicate whispers woven within the fabric of existence. It's in the gentle rustle of leaves, the caress of a breeze, or the fleeting moment of serenity found in a quiet sunrise. These subtle whispers carry the essence of guidance, offering profound insights and nudges from the realm beyond the tangible. Tuning into these whispers requires a quiet mind and an open heart, inviting a communion with the divine within the ordinary. It's in these understated moments that the universe speaks, offering guidance, solace, and a profound sense of interconnectedness, nurturing a spiritual resonance that transcends the boundaries of the physical world. Make your ordinary extraordinary, even if it's just for today.

21

Trust Yourself Enough To Take the Next Step

Life's journey often unfolds along a winding road, veering through unforeseen twists and turns, punctuated by moments of uncertainty and clarity alike. Amidst this labyrinthine path, trusting oneself to take the next step becomes an anchor in navigating the unknown. It's an acknowledgement that while the road ahead may not always be clear, there exists an innate compass within, guiding towards the next chapter. Embracing this trust in oneself isn't about having all the answers or avoiding stumbles; rather, it's about summoning the courage to step forward despite the ambiguity. It's a testament to self-belief and resilience, recognizing that each step, even if veering off the expected course, contributes to the richness of one's journey.

This trust instills the confidence to adapt, pivot, and course-correct along the way. It's an invitation to listen to the whispers of intuition and the inner voice urging forward momentum. While the road may curve unexpectedly, this trust in oneself becomes a steadfast companion, encouraging exploration, resilience, and the unwavering belief that every step, however uncertain, leads toward personal evolution and a more fulfilling destination. Trust your journey.

22

*D*on't Look Back

Closing the door and steadfastly refusing to look back embodies an act of unwavering resolve and self-preservation. It's an embodiment of courage, a testament to the strength found within, urging forward movement despite the allure of nostalgia or the temptation to dwell in the past. It's a decisive step toward embracing the unknown, acknowledging that some chapters, no matter how deeply cherished or intricately woven into our story, must reach their conclusion. Closing that door isn't an act of disregard for the memories or lessons learned, but rather a profound acknowledgment of the need to honor oneself, protect one's peace, and march boldly towards new horizons. It's about daring to carve a path where the echoes of yesterday fade into the distance, creating space for the whispers of tomorrow's possibilities to beckon, guiding toward a future where growth, resilience, and unwavering hope are waiting patiently for you.

23

You Owe It to Yourself to Become Everything You Dream of Becoming

You owe it to yourself to embrace the full spectrum of your aspirations and potentials, transcending the boundaries of doubt and fear. It's a commitment to nurturing the seeds of your dreams, allowing them to sprout and flourish into the magnificent tapestry of your reality. Each dream, no matter how grand or seemingly unattainable, carries within it the spark of possibility. By dedicating yourself to these aspirations, you honor the depth of your desires, affirming the belief that within you lies the capacity to manifest and embody the visions that stir your soul. Embracing this commitment is an acknowledgment of your worthiness—to live a life shaped by passion, purpose, and the unwavering pursuit of everything you've ever dared to dream.

Keep dreaming.

24

In The Story of Your Life, You Are the Hero

In the soulful tale of your life, a hero emerges with every line penned, every page turned, and every chapter lived. This hero, though not fully unveiled until the final pages of this narrative, embodies resilience, courage, and unwavering determination. As the story reaches its conclusion, you stand at the precipice of retrospection, gazing back with an embrace of love, grace, and boundless compassion. You behold every trial, every tribulation, and every challenge overcome—moments where companions stood by your side or when you stood valiantly alone. In this reflection, each struggle reveals itself as a testament to your strength, each triumph a testament to your resilience, painting a portrait of a hero who navigated the labyrinth of life with unwavering grace and a heart brimming with compassion. You are the hero of your own story.

25

This Is Just a Season, Stay Present There Are Lessons to Be Learned And Room to Grow

Amidst life's ever-changing seasons, the wisdom lies in staying rooted in the present moment. This joy, grief, love or excitement is fleeting yet potent. There are whispers of invaluable lessons waiting to be embraced and growth eager to spread its wings. It's a reminder that this moment isn't just a passing breeze but a crucial chapter in the journey of becoming. By immersing oneself in the here and now, one can glean the pearls of wisdom strewn within these fleeting moments. There's ample space for learning, for evolution, and for the nurturing of seeds that promise bountiful growth. Embracing this season with a presence of mind unveils the hidden gems within, offering rich experiences that foster resilience, wisdom, love and an unwavering spirit ready to blossom in the seasons yet to come.

26

*S*eeing With Fresh Eyes
Leads To Transformations

Viewing the world with fresh eyes is the catalyst for profound transformations. It's about shedding the filters of familiarity and opening oneself to the infinite possibilities veiled within the everyday. When we embrace this shift in perspective, the mundane becomes a canvas of untapped potential. Familiar landscapes reveal hidden wonders, routine experiences sparkle with newfound significance, and even the simplest moments whisper tales of untold beauty. Seeing things anew isn't just about optics; it's an internal rebirth, a recalibration of perception that invites innovative thoughts and novel solutions. It's in this reimagining that the seeds of transformation are sown, sprouting tendrils of creativity, curiosity, and a renewed sense of wonder that guide us towards uncharted realms of growth and evolution.

27

Transformation Begins With The Acceptance of What Is

Transformation spreads its wings upon the foundation of acceptance—embracing the raw truth of what exists in the present moment. It's about peering unflinchingly into the mirror of reality, acknowledging the nuances of one's circumstances, emotions, and experiences. This acceptance isn't resignation; rather, it's a catalyst for metamorphosis. It invites a dialogue with the self, fostering a profound understanding of the terrain upon which change can take root. By embracing what is, one lays the groundwork for evolution, drawing upon the essence of the present as a canvas to craft a future imbued with intention and purpose. It's in this acceptance that the seeds of transformation are sown, nurturing the fertile ground from which growth, resilience, and profound personal evolution blossom forth.

28

Dear Humans, You Are Love

Dear Humans,

The truth is you can't truly disconnect from the love that defines your essence. It's an inherent part of your being, an unbreakable thread that weaves through the fabric of your soul and your existence. Love isn't an external force you acquire or relinquish; it's the very essence of your nature. Even in moments of solitude or hardship, the pulse of love persists within, resilient and unwavering. Embracing this profound reality allows you to navigate life with compassion, resilience, and a deep understanding that, at your core, you are a manifestation of love itself. So, dear humans, acknowledge this eternal connection to love, both within and around you, and let it guide your journey with grace and authenticity.

29

Blending The Human Soul
Into The Eternal Spirit

Our human experiences serve as the alchemy that seamlessly blends the transient hues of the human soul into the timeless canvas of the eternal spirit. Each joy, sorrow, triumph, and challenge becomes a stroke in this intricate masterpiece of existence. It is through the prism of diverse emotions, connections, and journeys that the soul awakens to its eternal nature. The laughter shared, tears shed, and lessons learned weave a tapestry of wisdom that transcends the temporal. In these moments, the boundaries between the human soul and the eternal spirit blur, revealing an interconnected dance that echoes across the vast expanse of existence.

Our temporary earthly stay becomes the crucible where the soul refines, evolves, and ultimately merges with the eternal, shaping a narrative that resonates through the corridors of eternity.

30

It's Always Darkest Before the Light Keep Going!

Throughout our lives, we often find solace in the age-old adage that it's always darkest before the light. This enduring wisdom encapsulates the resilience embedded within our human experiences and our soul. Just when challenges seem insurmountable, and shadows loom large, it is precisely in those moments that the potential for transformation and renewal is most profound. The contrast between darkness and light serves as a poignant reminder that, even in our bleakest hours, the promise of dawn lingers on the horizon. Embracing this perspective allows us to navigate adversity with unwavering hope, recognizing that within the ebb and flow of life, the brilliance of a new beginning awaits. Today is your dawn!

31

On A Soul Level
Every Moment of Your Life Matters

In the grand journey of existence, every fleeting moment weaves a unique thread into the fabric of our lives. Each heartbeat, every breath drawn, and every step taken holds profound significance. It's a reminder that every moment matters—like a mosaic of experiences that shape the intricate portrait of who we are. In the ordinary and extraordinary alike, there lies the potential for growth, connection, and profound joy. Cherishing the present moment allows us to appreciate the beauty inherent in our journey and recognizing that, collectively, these moments compose the masterpiece of a life well-lived. So, embrace the richness of each passing second, for it is in the now that the true essence of our existence unfolds.

32

Memories Of Heaven
The Light Came from Within

In my memories of heaven, the ethereal glow emanates not from an external source but from within the very core of our being and all that is. It's a celestial radiance that transcends the confines of earthly experiences, illuminating everything in existence with a divine light. These memories, bathed in the warmth of blissful love, evoke a sense of profound connection and serenity. As I move through the landscape of recollections, each moment becomes a beacon, guiding me through the vast expanse of our personal cosmos. The light from within, born of heavenly impressions, leaves an indelible mark on my soul, reminding me that even in the earthly journey, there exists a touch of the divine that transcends time and space.

33

This Life Is the Dream

In the enigmatic dance of existence, our human experience unfolds as the dream we intricately weave through the fabric of eternity. Each moment, every emotion, and the kaleidoscope of interactions form the threads of this ethereal tapestry. As we navigate the realms of joy, sorrow, love, and discovery, the dreamlike quality of our journey becomes apparent. In the fluidity of life's transitions, we awaken to the realization that the boundaries between waking reality and the dream are permeable. Our human experience, with its myriad sensations and evolving narratives, embodies the essence of a dream—sometimes surreal, occasionally tumultuous, but always an immersive exploration of the profound depths of our existence. May you find peace as your soul continues this dream.

34

Light Workers
You Are Being Called into Action Now

Light Workers as bearers of spiritual illumination and
healing energies, they stand poised at the forefront of
transformative change. This pivotal moment calls upon
their innate gifts to inspire hope, foster compassion, and
ignite positive shifts in consciousness. Like beacons in
times of darkness, Light Workers emerge as catalysts for
collective awakening, guiding others towards
understanding, unity, and the radiance within. The
world, in its complexity, beckons these luminous souls
to illuminate the path of compassion, reminding us all
that even amidst challenges, the light they bring has the
power to illuminate the way forward.

35

Just For Today

Just for today, I choose to fully embrace and feel every emotion that courses through me. By allowing myself this authenticity, I lay the groundwork for a brighter tomorrow.

Tomorrow, I will step forward with a heart brimming with love, having navigated today's emotions as stepping stones toward growth and understanding. It's a commitment to live in the present, acknowledging that by honoring my feelings today, I cultivate a compassionate and resilient foundation for the beautiful journey that lies ahead. Just for today.

36

The Gift of Time

Time is an extraordinary gift, a canvas on which the story of our lives is painted. Each second, minute, and hour is a treasure, an opportunity to create, love, learn, and grow. Time allows us to cherish moments with loved ones, to heal from pain, and to celebrate joys. It's the quiet observer of our greatest achievements and our simplest pleasures. With every tick of the clock, time gives us the chance to change, to dream, and to become who we are meant to be. In its relentless passage, time teaches us the value of now – the precious present where life unfolds in its most authentic beauty. Let us embrace time not as a fleeting resource but as a heartfelt gift, reminding us to live each moment to its fullest.

37

Love Is Not a Place or a Person It's An Energy

Love is an energy that surpasses the bounds of time and space. This powerful, ethereal force connects us in ways that defy physical limitations, weaving through our lives as an unseen yet deeply felt presence. It is the invisible thread that binds the fabric of our experiences, enduring through shifts and changes, unaltered by distance or years. Love's energy resonates within and around us, a timeless, boundless essence that speaks to the core of our being, reminding us that its true nature lies in its ability to transcend the tangible and manifest in countless, ineffable ways.

38

The Hardest Part Is Letting Go

The act of letting go, often the most challenging part of our journey, is paradoxically where we find our greatest strength and freedom. It's in the release of what no longer serves us - be it a belief, a relationship, or a past self - that we make room for new growth and possibilities. Letting go is not a surrender, but a courageous act of trust in the journey of life. It opens us up to new horizons and allows us to embrace change as an integral part of our personal evolution. In this difficult process, we discover the transformative power of release, learning that in the space created by letting go, we find the seeds of new beginnings, hope, and an unexplored future brimming with potential. Just for today, let go.

39

We Don't Break Open So That the Light Can Get In, We Break Open So That the World Can See Our Inner Light

The notion that we break open not for the light to enter us, but rather to reveal our inner light to the world, is a profound perspective on personal growth and vulnerability. This idea suggests that our moments of struggle, pain, and breaking are not merely about allowing external wisdom or light to seep into our beings, but more about exposing the luminous, inherent strength and beauty that resides within us.

When we break open, it's as if the cracks in our armor become channels through which our deepest virtues – resilience, compassion, wisdom – are displayed for the world to see. It's a transformative process where what was once perceived as weakness becomes a beacon of hope and inspiration for others, a testament to the indomitable spirit that glows within each of us. In this way, our trials and tribulations are not just personal journeys but also gifts to the world, as they allow our inner light to shine forth and illuminate the paths of those around us.

40

Finding Your Soul's True North

Finding your soul's true north is a journey of profound self-discovery and alignment with your deepest values and aspirations. It's akin to navigating the vast oceans of life guided by an internal compass that points towards your most authentic self. This journey requires introspection, courage, and a willingness to venture beyond the familiar territories of comfort and conformity.

As you listen intently to the whispers of your heart and the callings of your spirit, you gradually peel away the layers of societal expectations, fears, and doubts, uncovering the essence of who you truly are. In finding your true north, you find a path that resonates with your core, a direction that leads to fulfillment, purpose, and a sense of peace. It's not just about reaching a destination, but about embracing the journey, learning from each step, and growing in wisdom and strength. When you align with your soul's true north, you move through life with greater authenticity, making decisions and forging relationships that deeply honor your true self, and in doing so, you light the way for others to find their own paths.

41

As The Fog Lifts

Emerging from an emotional fog is akin to the first rays of dawn piercing through a dense, grey mist, bringing clarity and light to a once obscured world. It's a gradual awakening, where each moment of lucidity feels like a breath of fresh air, invigorating the soul. This lifting of the fog represents a significant turning point, a gentle yet profound shift from confusion and uncertainty to a clearer understanding of oneself and one's path. It's as if the mental and emotional clutter that clouded judgment and dampened spirits begins to disperse, revealing a landscape of possibilities that was always there, just hidden from view.

In this newfound clarity, there's a sense of renewal and hope, a belief that challenges can be navigated and joy can be rediscovered. Each step out of the fog is a step towards a stronger, more resilient self, armed with the wisdom gleaned from the journey through the haze. As the fog lifts, it leaves behind a clearer, brighter horizon, a promise that even in our darkest times, there is always a path leading back to light.

Take the next step on your path to the light.

42

Every Prayer We Pray Has Been Prayed Before

The idea that every prayer we utter has been echoed in the past weaves a profound tapestry of spiritual continuity, binding us across time and space in a shared human experience. When we bow our heads, close our eyes, and whisper our hopes, fears, and gratitude, we are not alone; we are part of an immense chorus of souls who have uttered similar "please" and "thank you". Our prayers, in their sincerity and hope, amplify the resonances of those that came before us, creating a powerful symphony of collective yearning and faith.

Similarly, the prayers of the past lend strength and depth to our own, as if each word we speak is bolstered by the weight of countless others who have sought the same comfort, guidance, or grace. This beautiful interplay of voices, transcending time and uniting us in our most vulnerable moments, serves as a reminder of our shared humanity, our interconnectedness, and the timeless nature of our spiritual quests. In this act of prayer, no matter how solitary it may seem, we find a profound unity, an affirmation that in our deepest hopes and fears, we are truly all one.

43

The Journey of Becoming

Not being who you once were encapsulates the beautiful evolution intrinsic to the human experience. It signifies shedding layers of the past—old beliefs, outdated perceptions, and former versions of oneself—to make space for growth and transformation. It's a testament to the resilience of the human spirit, acknowledging that each experience, triumph, and setback contributes to the ongoing narrative of self-discovery. Embracing this change isn't about discarding the past but rather honoring it as a crucial chapter in the journey of becoming. It's recognizing the continual process of reinvention, understanding that every moment offers the opportunity to rewrite the script, allowing the authentic self to emerge in its ever-unfolding glory. Not being who you once were is a celebration of the dynamic nature of existence and the endless possibilities inherent in embracing change.

44

Never Alone

Throughout our journey through life, we are never truly alone, even in moments when solitude feels all-encompassing. Along this intricate path, we are accompanied by the whispers of our angels, life guides & loved ones in Spirit, the strength drawn from the memories of the past, and the invisible presence of those who have touched our lives, however briefly. Friends, family, mentors, and even strangers contribute to the rich tapestry of our existence, offering guidance, support, and companionship. Their influence shapes our character, molds our perspectives, and propels us forward. Moreover, the digital age has woven a web of connectivity, ensuring that physical distance no longer equates to isolation. Thus, in the grand narrative of our lives, every encounter, every connection, serves as a reminder that we navigate this journey amidst a constellation of souls, each one a beacon, reminding us that we are, in essence, never alone.

45

Mediumship Helpful Tips

Mediumship, often perceived as a "mystical gift" reserved for the few, is actually a universal connection that everyone has the potential to tap into, bridging the gap between the physical world and the spiritual realm. This conduit of communication opens the door to heartfelt interactions with departed loved ones, providing comfort and continued bonds that transcend the limitations of the physical world. Furthermore, it serves as a gateway to receiving guidance and support from angels and life guides, who watch over us and steer us towards our life's purpose.

Engaging with these spiritual entities can enrich our lives, offering insights, peace, and a deeper understanding of the universe's interconnectedness. As individuals explore and nurture their innate abilities to connect with the spiritual realm, they discover that mediumship is not just an exclusive skill but a shared, universal tool.

46

When You Are in the Flow with Life Things Happen Effortlessly

When in sync with the flow of life, existence seems to harmonize effortlessly. It's like gliding downstream with the current, where actions unfold seamlessly, and opportunities unfurl naturally.

In this state, there's a magnetic resonance between intention and manifestation, as if the universe conspires to pave the way for your endeavors. Decisions align effortlessly, obstacles dissolve or gently nudge you in a different direction, and serendipitous moments seem to dot the path. Being in the flow doesn't imply an absence of challenges but rather a sense of alignment that allows for a smoother navigation through life's ebbs and flows. It's a state of being where intuition serves as a compass, guiding choices, and circumstances seem to effortlessly fall into place, affirming that sometimes, the most magical moments unfold when we surrender and allow life's rhythm to carry us forward.

47

Trust The Process of Your Divine Path

Trusting the process of your divine path is an act of faith, a surrender to the unseen forces that guide your journey through life. It requires an unwavering belief in the notion that every twist, turn, and obstacle encountered is a part of a larger plan, intricately designed for your ultimate growth and fulfillment. Embracing this path means acknowledging that the moments of uncertainty and challenge are not deviations but essential chapters of your story, each with a purpose and a lesson to impart. It's about understanding that the timing of events, the people we meet, and the experiences we undergo are aligned with a greater wisdom than we can comprehend.

Trusting this process involves letting go of the need to control every outcome, instead moving forward with a heart open to possibilities and a spirit willing to accept and learn from whatever comes your way. It's a journey of continuous discovery, where faith in your divine path becomes the light that guides you through darkness, the anchor in times of storm, and the compass that leads you to your true north, revealing the beauty and strength that lie within.

48

*I*ntuition
The Whisper That Turns into a Roar

Intuition is often likened to a whisper, a subtle, almost imperceptible nudge from within that guides us in moments of uncertainty. This whisper, quiet yet persistent, is born from a deep well of wisdom, a culmination of our experiences, emotions, and unspoken knowledge. As we learn to listen and trust this inner voice, the whisper grows, gaining clarity and strength, until it becomes a roar—an undeniable force that guides our decisions and actions with an almost primal certainty.

This transformation from a whisper to a roar is not just about recognizing intuition but also about embracing it with confidence. It becomes a powerful ally in navigating life's complexities, often leading us down paths we might not have logically chosen, yet which resonate profoundly with our core. In tuning into this intuitive roar, we find ourselves more aligned with our true selves, making choices that are authentic and right for us, and often, by extension, for those around us. Intuition, in its loudest form, is a reminder of the extraordinary capability we have to understand and navigate our world beyond the limits of rational thought.

49

We Open Like a Rose

Like a rose delicately unfurling its petals to the warmth of the sun, we too open in layers, each one revealing a deeper part of our essence. This process of blossoming is not one of haste but of gentle, patient unveiling, where every layer holds its own beauty and complexity. With each petal that opens, we expose vulnerabilities and strengths, fears and dreams, weaving the intricate story of who we are. Just as the rose does not bloom all at once, our opening is a journey, influenced by the light and shadows of our experiences, the nourishment of love and the trials of pain. It's a natural, graceful progression towards our fullest expression, where we become more accessible to the world and to ourselves, sharing the fragrance of our being with those who dare to come close.

In this vulnerability, there's a profound strength, for as we open like a rose, we invite connections that are most authentic, creating bonds that are rooted in the true depth of our souls.

50

Your Loved Ones on The Other Side Are Watching Over You

Our loved ones in Spirit continue to assist us from the other side. Now free from earthly limitations, they offer us guidance, protection, and encouragement through the subtleties of our intuition, dreams, and seemingly coincidental occurrences. They are watching over us, sending signs and messages that, if we are open and attentive, can provide comfort, reassurance, and sometimes direction during our most challenging moments. This ongoing support is a testament to the enduring nature of love and the interconnectedness of all life. In our journey through life, we are accompanied not just by the seen but also by the unseen forces of those who have loved us and continue to do so from beyond the physical realm.

51

Dig Deeper
You've Got This!

In those moments when the urge to quit whispers seductively, tempting you to lay down your dreams and walk away, it's crucial to summon the strength to dig deeper into yourself. These challenging times are not the signals to retreat but to reach further into the reservoirs of grit and determination that reside within you. Remember, you didn't embark on this journey, overcoming obstacles and pushing past limits, only to stop at the brink of your breakthrough. Every step you've taken has been a testament to your resilience, a building block of your growth.

This moment, as daunting as it may seem, is no different. It's another opportunity to prove to yourself that your spirit is indomitable, that your capacity for perseverance outmatches any temptation to give up. Let the knowledge of how far you've come be the wind beneath your wings, propelling you forward. For on the other side of this struggle lies not just the achievement of your goals, but the realization of your potential to surpass every expectation you once set for yourself. You didn't come this far only to come this far; you came this far to fly, dream and achieve.

52

Your Deepest Pain Can Launch You on The Path to Your Greatest Calling

There are moments in life when the depths of despair seem to engulf us, moments so dark that we question the very purpose of our pain. Yet, it is often within these harrowing depths that the seeds of our greatest calling are sown by the divine. Our most profound suffering can be a powerful catalyst for transformation and growth. Through our trials, we are shaped, our resilience is tested, and our true strength emerges. It is in navigating these trials that we often find our purpose, a calling that not only heals our own wounds but also lights the way for others struggling through their darkness.

This divine orchestration reveals that our greatest pains are not the end of our story but, rather, the beginning of a new, meaningful chapter, where our deepest struggles become the foundation of our most significant contributions to the world.

53

There Is a Calmness That Comes When We Realize It's Time to Move Forward

There exists a profound sense of calmness that envelops us when we reach the pivotal realization that it's time to move forward. This moment, often born from periods of turmoil, uncertainty, or introspection, marks a significant turning point in our lives. It's as if the stormy seas within us suddenly still, allowing us to see our path ahead with newfound clarity. This tranquility stems from the acceptance of change, the release of what no longer serves us, and the embracing of new possibilities. It's a serene acknowledgment that the past, with all its lessons and hardships, has prepared us for the next chapter. Moving forward then becomes not just an action, but a manifestation of our growth, resilience, and the quiet strength that comes from knowing we are ready to embrace the future, whatever it may hold.

54

The Storm

The person who emerges from the storm does not bear the same countenance as the one who first stepped into its tempest. This transformation, wrought by the tumult and turbulence of the storm, carves depths into the soul and etches wisdom into the heart. Through the howling winds and relentless rains, amidst the thunder that shakes the spirit and lightning that illuminates fears, an evolution occurs. The ordeal strips away layers of pretense, reveals strengths previously unknown, and often forces a confrontation with vulnerabilities. It is a profound metamorphosis, where resilience is forged in the crucible of adversity, and a new sense of self is born from the struggle. This rebirth, this emergence from the storm, signifies not just survival but a deeper, more meaningful growth.

The individual who steps out into the calm after the storm is richer in spirit, tempered by trials, and fundamentally transformed. They carry with them the indelible marks of their journey, a testament to their endurance and a beacon of hope for others who might find themselves facing their own tempests.

55

Passing By Suicide

In the wake of a loss by suicide, it's essential to remember that those who pass in such profound despair are still enfolded in the boundless love of God/Source/The Divine. The notion that a loving Creator extends compassion and understanding beyond our earthly judgments offers comfort and solace to those grappling with such tragedies.

God/Source/The Divine represents love that is pure and unconditional, transcending the circumstances of death and embracing every soul with empathy and grace. It is a reminder that our human understanding of spiritual matters is limited, but the divine capacity for love is infinite. In this light, we are encouraged to know that those who leave us by suicide find peace in the arms of a loving Source, who sees the depths of their pain and welcomes them into a realm of eternal love and healing.

56

You Can Make the World A Little Brighter and Kinder

Within every heart lies an untapped reservoir of kindness, a potential to cast light in the shadows of the world with the simplest of actions. This reminder, gentle yet powerful, calls us to recognize our own capacity to effect change, not through grand gestures, but through the everyday acts of compassion and empathy. It's in the warmth of a genuine smile, the patience in listening, the willingness to understand, and the courage to offer a hand. Each small deed is a testament to the goodness inherent in us, a single spark that can ignite hope and joy in others. As these sparks multiply, they weave a tapestry of kindness, brightening the world around us. It's a reminder that the journey to a kinder world begins within each of us, one act at a time, proving that even the smallest gesture can echo endlessly in the hearts and lives it touches.

57

Refuse To Settle

Refusing to settle for less than you deserve echoes a profound self-respect that permeates every aspect of life, especially in relationships and work. In romantic partnerships, it's about cherishing a connection that honors your worth—a relationship that nurtures mutual growth, respect, and unwavering support. It's choosing a partner who sees your essence, appreciates your quirks, and uplifts your spirit, fostering a bond built on love, understanding, and shared aspirations. Similarly, in friendships, it's surrounding yourself with individuals who cherish your authenticity, celebrate your victories, and stand by you through trials. These friendships enrich your life, offering camaraderie and support, rooted in trust and genuine care.

In the realm of work, it's about pursuing a vocation that ignites your passion, values your contributions, and offers room for growth and fulfillment. It's daring to seek an environment that aligns with your values, leverages your strengths, and acknowledges your potential, fostering a professional journey imbued with purpose and satisfaction. Refusing to settle stems from recognizing your inherent worth, paving the way for a life colored by meaningful connections and endeavors that resonate with the truest essence of who you are.

58

With Every Goodbye We Learn

With every goodbye, whether simple or laden with complexity, we embark on a profound journey of learning and self-discovery. These farewells, though often accompanied by a blend of sorrow and uncertainty, serve as crucial junctures in our lives, teaching us resilience, the impermanence of moments, and the enduring strength of our connections. A simple goodbye can remind us to cherish the present, highlighting the beauty of fleeting encounters. In contrast, a complicated goodbye challenges us to navigate the intricacies of human emotions, relationships, and the often-painful process of letting go. Both scenarios, however different, equip us with deeper wisdom, empathy, and a greater understanding of our own capacity for growth and renewal. Thus, each goodbye, no matter its nature, is an invitation to reflect, to learn, and ultimately, to evolve.

59

You've Got This!

Trusting in yourself is the cornerstone of achieving your goals. It's a silent affirmation that whispers, "You've got this", even when the odds seem stacked against you. This self-assured confidence doesn't shout; it's a quiet knowing, a steady flame in the darkness guiding your way. When you trust yourself, you tap into a reservoir of inner strength and wisdom that has been accumulating with every experience, every failure, and every triumph. It's recognizing that you are your most reliable ally, equipped with all the tools needed to navigate life's journey.

Embrace this trust, and let it propel you forward. Challenge the doubts, face the fears, and remember that you are capable, resilient, and deserving of your dreams. With self-trust as your foundation, there's nothing you can't achieve. You've indeed got this, not just for today, but for all the days to come.

60

Being The Light

Being the light in a world that often feels shrouded in darkness is a profound calling. It means illuminating the paths of others with kindness, hope, and compassion, even when your own journey feels uncertain. To be the light is to embrace the power within you to spark change, to warm the hearts of those around you, and to guide them through their darkest hours. It's about finding the courage to shine brightly, not just for yourself, but for the collective good, inspiring others to ignite their inner luminance along the way. Remember, even the smallest flame can pierce the night, transforming shadows into guides. By choosing to be the light, you become a beacon of resilience and a testament to the boundless strength of the human spirit. Let your light shine unapologetically, for it is in sharing your glow that you illuminate the world.

61

What Do You Really Want?

Asking yourself, "What do I really want?" is an act of self-discovery and empowerment. It's about peeling back the layers of expectations, obligations, and societal norms to uncover the deepest desires of your heart. In this question lies the key to unlocking your truest passions, dreams, and aspirations. It's an invitation to tune into your innermost desires, to listen to the whispers of your soul, and to pursue a path that aligns with your authentic self. Embrace this question as a beacon of clarity amidst life's complexities, allowing it to guide you towards a life filled with purpose, fulfillment, and joy. Remember, your dreams are worthy of pursuit, and by daring to ask yourself what you truly want, you embark on a journey of self-discovery that leads to boundless possibilities.

62

If You Focus on the Lessons You Will Find Your Way

If you learn to focus on the lessons that life presents to you, navigating your path becomes a journey of profound growth and fulfillment. Every challenge, every setback, harbors a lesson waiting to be discovered, a silver lining designed to enrich your wisdom and guide your steps. By shifting your perspective to see these obstacles as opportunities for learning, you unlock the potential to transform your life's most difficult moments into stepping stones towards your dreams. This focus on lessons rather than losses cultivates resilience, empowers positive change, and aligns your actions with your highest aspirations. With each lesson embraced, you'll find yourself moving closer to your true purpose, confidently navigating the winding roads of life, assured that you will indeed find your way.

63

Trust In the Magic of The Universe

Quit giving The Universe a million reasons for why the prayer in your heart "can't" work out. Instead, let your faith be the unwavering force that propels you forward, even when the path ahead seems uncertain. Believe in the power of your dreams, for they are the seeds of possibility waiting to bloom into reality. Trust in the divine timing of The Universe, knowing that every setback is merely a detour leading you closer to your ultimate destination. Embrace each challenge as an opportunity to strengthen your resolve and deepen your connection to the guiding forces of the cosmos.

Remember, The Universe conspires in your favor, always ready to align with your highest good. So, release the doubts, quiet the fears, and allow your heart's desires to manifest with unwavering faith. You are capable of miracles beyond your wildest imagination— trust in the magic of The Universe and watch as your prayers unfold in magnificent ways.

64

Stand In Your Power
Beautiful Soul

Stand in your power, beautiful soul, for within you lies an infinite reservoir of strength, courage, and resilience. Embrace the fullness of who you are, honoring your unique gifts and embracing your authentic self without hesitation. Let your light shine brightly, illuminating the world with your presence and inspiring others to do the same. Trust in your intuition, for it is the compass that guides you towards your true purpose and deepest desires. With every step you take, know that you are capable of achieving greatness and making a profound impact on the world around you. Embrace your power with grace and confidence, knowing that you are worthy of all the love, joy, and abundance that the universe has to offer. You are a radiant being of light, and the world is infinitely brighter because you are in it.

65

Believe In Yourself

Believing in yourself and the gifts that have been bestowed upon you is the ultimate act of faith and gratitude. It's about recognizing the unique talents and abilities that make you who you are and trusting in their divine purpose. As you embrace these gifts with humility and reverence, you align yourself with the infinite wisdom of the universe, knowing that you are a vessel for light, grace and love. With unwavering faith in your potential, you have the power to overcome any obstacle, fulfill your deepest dreams, and leave a lasting impact on the world. So, stand tall in the knowledge that you are perfectly and wonderfully created, and let your light shine brightly for all to see.

66

Raise Your Standards

Dare to demand excellence in all aspects of your life, from your relationships to your career, your health, and beyond. As you elevate your expectations, you signal to the universe that you are ready to receive its blessings in abundance. Trust in the power of your intentions, knowing that when you aim for the stars, the universe conspires to make your dreams a reality. So, refuse to settle for anything less than you deserve, and watch as the universe unfolds its magic to fulfill your highest aspirations.

67

Make A Wish

Making a wish is like planting a seed in the fertile soil of the universe, trusting in the unseen forces to bring it to fruition. It's about summoning the courage to dream boldly and envision a future filled with endless possibilities. Yet, the true magic lies not just in making the wish, but in releasing it to the flow of life's infinite potential. Allow your wish to take flight on the wings of faith, knowing that every step you take is guided by the universe's gentle hand. Embrace the uncertainty, the twists and turns of the journey, for it is in these moments that life's true magic unfolds. Surrender to the rhythm of the universe, and watch as your wish blossoms into reality, each moment infused with the enchanting glow of possibility. So, dare to make your wish, and then let go, trusting in the universe to weave its intricate tapestry of miracles to bring it to life.

68

The Bridge Will Appear

Life is a journey adorned with countless bridges, each one leading us closer to our aspirations and dreams. These bridges span the chasms of doubt and fear, connecting us to the possibilities that lie beyond. With each step we take, we traverse these bridges, crossing over obstacles and challenges, propelled by the vision of our deepest desires. Along the way, we encounter opportunities and lessons, each one a stepping stone towards the fulfillment of our aspirations. These bridges remind us that no dream is too distant, no goal too lofty, for with persistence and determination, we can bridge the gap between where we are and where we long to be. So, let us embrace the journey, knowing that every bridge we cross brings us closer to the realization of our dreams, and every challenge we overcome strengthens our resolve to reach them.

69

Your Purpose Is To Fully Be Who You Are

Your purpose in life is to be authentically, unapologetically, and fully yourself. Embrace every facet of your being—the light and the shadows, the triumphs and the challenges. For it is in honoring your true essence that you radiate your brightest light, inspire others to do the same, and fulfill your soul's deepest calling. So, dare to be yourself, fiercely and fearlessly, for in doing so, you unlock the door to boundless joy, fulfillment, and meaning in your journey through life.

70

Discovering What Makes You Truly Happy

It's about tuning into the whispers of your heart, embracing the activities, experiences, and relationships that ignite your soul with joy and fulfillment. Whether it's a simple moment of solitude in nature, a heartfelt conversation with a loved one, or pursuing your passions with unwavering determination, honoring what brings you happiness is a sacred act of self-love. Trust in your instincts, follow your bliss, and allow yourself to bask in the radiant glow of your own happiness. For when you prioritize your happiness, you unlock the door to a life filled with purpose, meaning, and boundless joy. May you discover true happiness!

71

It's Time to Thrive

It's time to thrive—to embrace the fullness of life with courage, determination, and unwavering optimism. Release the shackles of doubt and fear, and step boldly into the brilliance of your own potential. Seize each moment as an opportunity for growth, learning, and transformation, and let your inner light shine brightly for all to see. Embrace challenges as stepping stones to success, and trust in your ability to overcome any obstacle that stands in your way. Now is the time to unleash your true greatness, to live with purpose, passion, and unyielding resilience. So, spread your wings and soar, for the world awaits the magnificent contributions only you can offer. It's time to thrive.

72

*D*ream Bigger

Dream bigger, for the canvas of your potential knows no bounds. Within each of you lies a spark of divine creativity, a flame that illuminates the path to your highest aspirations. See yourselves as worthy, cherished, and infinitely capable of greatness. Let your dreams soar beyond the confines of doubt and limitation and embrace the inherent worth that resides within your soul. For in daring to believe in yourselves, you unlock the door to a world of limitless possibilities, where your wildest dreams become reality, and your light shines brightly for all to see. Dream big, dear ones, and watch as the tapestry of your destiny unfolds with beauty, purpose, and boundless love.

73

Who Am I Now?

Humans are ever-evolving beings, shaped by experiences, choices, and the passage of time. As we navigate the complexities of life, we undergo transformations, shedding old identities and embracing new ones. In the pursuit of self-discovery, we often find ourselves asking, "Who am I now?" This question serves as a catalyst for growth, prompting introspection and self-awareness. With each iteration of ourselves, we uncover hidden strengths, passions, and truths, carving out a path towards authenticity and fulfillment. Embrace the journey of change, for it is through this metamorphosis that we truly discover the depths of our being and the limitless potential that resides within.

74

Be The Best Version of Yourself And Know That You Are Needed In This World

Be the best version of yourself—not the perfect version, but the true, brave, evolving you. Every day is an opportunity to grow, to learn, and to step more fully into who you were meant to be. Remember, you were not placed in this world by accident. Your light, your voice, your presence—*they matter*. Even on the days you doubt your worth, know that you are needed more than you realize. Keep shining, even if it's just a flicker. The world is brighter because you're in it.

Keep shining!

75

Everyone Has a Guardian Angel

During earthly life, each of us is accompanied by at least one guardian angel, unseen yet ever-present, guiding us through both triumphs and trials. These celestial beings are the embodiment of love, protection, and divine intervention, tirelessly watching over us with unwavering devotion. Whether in moments of joy or despair, they whisper messages of hope, nudging us towards paths of light and purpose. Though their presence may go unnoticed, their influence is profound, weaving miracles into the fabric of our existence. With every step we take, our guardian angels walk beside us, illuminating the way with their ethereal glow and reminding us that we are never alone on this journey called life.

76

Embrace This Moment

Embrace this moment in your life with a spirit of mindfulness and gratitude, for it is a precious gift waiting to be unwrapped. Be fully present, allowing yourself to immerse in the richness of each experience, the beauty of every breath, and the depth of every emotion. In the ever-flowing hourglass of time, this moment is uniquely yours, filled with endless possibilities and boundless potential. Seize it with courage and intention, for within it lies the power to shape your destiny and create the life of your dreams. Embrace the journey, cherish the memories, and live each moment with purpose and passion, for in doing so, you unlock the true essence of living.

77

Give Yourself Permission to Simply Be

Today, I grant myself the liberating gift of simply existing. Amidst the chaos of life's demands and expectations, I embrace the tranquility found in the act of being. I release the pressures of productivity and perfection, allowing myself to revel in the beauty of each moment as it unfolds. With each breath, I immerse myself in the present, finding solace in the awareness of my own existence. Today, I am free to be unapologetically myself, embracing my flaws and celebrating my strengths. This day is mine to savor, to cherish, and to simply be.

78

Love Lives On

The journey through grief is a sacred passage that each individual traverses in their own way and at their own pace. It's a profound, intricate labyrinth of emotions, thoughts, and experiences, leading you through the depths of loss and sorrow towards healing and transformation. It's a deeply personal expedition marked by unique memories, connections, and the intricate tapestry of the relationship once shared.

On this sacred journey, you are invited to honor a path where memories, emotions and even the mundane become imbued with significance, offering solace and a connection with your loved one in Spirit. The body does not continue on, but your love and connection does. Your loved one in Spirit is walking next to you every step of the way. Honor your sacred journey.

Love Lives On

79

Invest In Yourself

Investing time, energy, healing, and love in oneself is the ultimate act of self-care and empowerment. It's a journey of self-discovery and self-nurturing, where each moment dedicated to personal growth becomes a precious investment in one's well-being. By carving out time for self-reflection, practicing self-compassion, and prioritizing activities that nourish the soul, we replenish our energy reserves and cultivate a deeper sense of inner harmony. This process isn't just about indulgence; it's about building resilience, fostering self-awareness, and laying the foundation for a fulfilling life. As we tend to our own needs with tenderness and devotion, we unlock the boundless potential within us, radiating love and light into every corner of our existence.

80

Synchronicity

In the intricate dance of life, synchronicity unveils itself
as a divine symphony orchestrated by the universe.
Every seemingly random encounter, every serendipitous
moment, whispers the profound truth that we are not
alone but rather intricately connected to the vast
tapestry of existence. The universe, in its infinite
wisdom, gently guides us along our path, nudging us
toward the experiences, lessons, and connections that
our souls crave. With open hearts and minds, we
embrace the synchronicities that pepper our journey,
recognizing them as cosmic signposts affirming that we
are exactly where we are meant to be. In the grand
design of the cosmos, every moment is infused with
meaning, every step a testament to the universe's
unwavering guidance and boundless love.

81

Starting Over

Each day, our life starts over again, offering us a blank canvas to create anew. With the dawn of every morning, we are granted a fresh beginning, a chance to let go of past regrets and embrace the potential of the present. This daily renewal invites us to redefine our goals, rekindle our passions, and approach our challenges with renewed vigor. It is a reminder that no matter what has come before, we have the power to shape our future, moment by moment. Embrace each new day as a precious gift, filled with opportunities to grow, to love, and to make a difference. Let the promise of a new beginning inspire you to live fully and authentically, knowing that with each sunrise, you are given a beautiful chance to start again.

82

Make Peace with Yourself

Making peace with oneself is a sacred journey of self-acceptance and self-love. It's about releasing the chains of self-doubt and embracing the radiant truth of our inherent worthiness. No longer do we seek external validation or rely on others to define our sense of self; instead, we find solace in the depths of our own being. We recognize that our imperfections are what make us beautifully human, and we extend to ourselves the same compassion and kindness we offer to others. In the gentle embrace of self-acceptance, we let go of the need for perfection and honor the unique essence that defines us. We no longer search for reasons to feel unworthy but instead celebrate our strengths and honor our vulnerabilities as integral parts of our journey. With each step towards self-compassion, we reclaim our power, our authenticity, and our unwavering belief in our inherent worthiness.

83

Make The World a Better, Brighter Place

Each of us is a beautiful and powerful soul, imbued with unique qualities that light up the world in ways only we can. Our inner strength and beauty shine through our actions, our kindness, and our resilience in the face of adversity. We possess the power to inspire, to heal, and to transform not only our lives but also the lives of those around us. When we recognize and embrace our inherent worth and potential, we become unstoppable forces of good, capable of creating profound change. Let us celebrate our individual radiance and harness our power to make the world a better, brighter place.

84

Celebrating The Divine Mother

Celebrating the Divine Mother, we honor the extraordinary love of all moms, embracing those whose children play in Heaven with angels, those moms who now watch over us from realms beyond, and the devoted fur baby moms who nurture and cherish their beloved companions. To every mother, whether cradling a child in her arms or holding their soul close to her heart, your love knows no bounds. Your strength, resilience, and unwavering devotion illuminate the world with boundless warmth and compassion. Through every joy and every tear, you embody the essence of unconditional love, shaping lives with your tenderness and wisdom. We celebrate the profound impact you have made, the countless hearts you have touched, and the endless blessings you bestow upon us. The Divine Mother is in all moms, in every form and in every corner of the world. Your love is the heartbeat of humanity, and your presence is a gift beyond measure.

85

Heal Yourself

Embark on the journey to heal yourself, for within the depths of your being lies the key to unlocking a future filled with boundless light and possibility. As you tenderly tend to the wounds of your past, embracing forgiveness, self-compassion, and growth, you pave the way for a radiant tomorrow. Know that the universe stands beside you, a steadfast ally cheering you on with every step you take towards healing and wholeness. Embrace the transformative power that resides within you, allowing it to guide you towards a future where joy, abundance, and fulfillment await.

With each moment of self-discovery and self-care, you align yourself with the infinite potential of the cosmos, ready to embrace the bright future that beckons you forward. The universe rejoices in your courage and resilience, for in your healing, you not only transform yourself but also illuminate the path for others to follow.

86

Be Here Now

Allow yourself to be fully present today, embracing each moment with mindful awareness. Set aside the distractions of past regrets and future anxieties and focus on the here and now. Notice the details around you—the warmth of the sun, the sounds of nature, the rhythm of your breath. Engage deeply with the people you encounter, listening and responding with genuine attention. By grounding yourself in the present, you open the door to a richer, more meaningful experience of life, fostering a sense of peace and fulfillment that can only be found in the now.

87

In The Quiet Moments You Can Hear God Speak

In the quiet moments, when the hustle of life fades into the background, you can hear God speak. It's in these serene pauses that the whispers of the Divine become discernible, offering guidance, comfort, and wisdom. Away from the clamor and noise, your heart and mind become attuned to a deeper spiritual frequency. These moments of stillness allow you to reflect, pray, meditate and connect with a higher presence, revealing insights and truths that often go unnoticed in the busyness of daily life. Embracing these quiet times not only nurtures your soul but also strengthens your faith, reminding you of the ever-present companionship of the Spirit world.

88

Loved Ones in Spirit

Our loved ones in Spirit are always with us, surrounding us with their enduring presence and love. Though they may no longer walk beside us in the physical form, their essence remains intertwined with our lives. We sense their presence in the gentle breeze, the warmth of a memory, and the signs they send—like a familiar scent, a favorite song, or a timely coincidence. Their love transcends the boundaries of the physical realm, offering comfort and reassurance that we are never truly alone. By opening our hearts and minds to their spiritual presence, we can feel their unwavering support and guidance, reminding us that love is eternal and unbreakable, even across dimensions.

89

Find The Magic in Life

Finding magic in your life begins with embracing the wonder and beauty in everyday moments. It's about looking at the world with a sense of curiosity and awe, recognizing the extraordinary in the ordinary. Magic resides in the laughter shared with friends, the serenity of a sunrise, the kindness of a stranger, and the quiet moments of reflection. It's in pursuing your passions, dreaming boldly, and cherishing the connections that bring joy and meaning to your existence. By opening your heart to these experiences and allowing yourself to be fully present, you cultivate a life filled with enchantment and endless possibilities. Embrace the magic that surrounds you, and let it inspire you to live more fully and love more deeply.

90

Choose Peace Within

Choose to let peace live within, cultivating a sanctuary of calm and serenity in your heart. In a world often filled with chaos and noise, make a conscious decision to embrace tranquility and let it guide your actions and thoughts. By releasing the burdens of past hurts and future worries, you create space for inner harmony to flourish. Anchor yourself in the present moment, breathing deeply and finding solace in the simple beauty of life. This inner peace radiates outward, touching relationships and interactions with a gentle, soothing presence that will ripple throughout the world.

91

A Season of Endings

A season of endings leads to a season of new beginnings, reminding us that life is a continuous cycle of growth and renewal. While farewells and endings can be bittersweet, they pave the way for fresh starts and new opportunities. Each ending, whether it's a chapter in our lives, a relationship, or a phase of personal development, carries with it the seeds of transformation. As we let go of a version of us that no longer serves who we are now, we create space for new experiences and possibilities to flourish. Embrace the uncertainty and the promise of what lies ahead, knowing that every ending is a precursor to a beautiful new beginning. May your new beginnings be beautiful and full of love.

92

What If, Just for Today, You Surrender to the Conflict, Pain, And Chaos in Your Life?

What if, just for today, you surrender to the conflict, pain, and chaos in your life? What if, just for today, you choose peace, love, and joy over being right? What if, just for today, you assume that everything in your life is on track and working out for your highest good? What if, just for today, you assume that you are perfect in this moment, exactly as you are? How would you feel about your life then?

Your free will and freedom exist in this moment, in your perception.

Just for today...

93

You Are a Soul

You don't have a soul; you are a soul, and you have a body. This realization shifts our understanding of existence, reminding us that our true essence transcends the physical form. Our bodies are vessels that carry us through the earthly journey, but it is our soul that holds our deepest truths, passions, and eternal light. By recognizing ourselves as souls, we embrace a higher perspective that values inner growth, connection, and purpose over mere material existence. This awareness encourages us to nurture our spiritual well-being, honor our inner wisdom, and live authentically. Understanding this distinction empowers us to lead lives rich with meaning, compassion, and profound fulfillment.

94

The Ocean of Life

In the ocean of life, certainty lies in knowing that there will always be another wave. Some waves may feel crushing, leaving us gasping for breath, while others will offer a thrilling, joyous ride that lifts our spirits. This ever-changing sea is our school of life, where the goal is to learn to harmonize with each wave, embracing both the challenges and the triumphs. By cultivating resilience and balance, we can navigate the turbulent waters with grace and strength. Each wave, whether daunting or delightful, teaches us invaluable lessons and shapes our journey. Embrace the waves, trust in your ability to adapt, and find peace in the rhythmic ebb and flow of life's ocean.

95

Celebrating The Divine Father

Celebrate the Divine Father with hearts full of love. To the dads whose children are in heaven, your love transcends time and space, an eternal bond that nothing can break. To the dads watching us from above, your guidance and spirit remain our guiding light, your legacy living on in every cherished memory and your wisdom still guiding us. To the dads of fur babies, your nurturing care and companionship speak volumes of your boundless capacity to love. And to the dads who hold their children's hands through every step of life's journey, your unwavering presence and support shape the future in the most beautiful ways. Today, we honor and thank you for the endless love and strength you give.

96

The Time Is Now

The time is now. This is your moment to take that trip you've always dreamed of, to apply for the new job that excites your spirit, and to embrace a life you truly love. Don't wait for the perfect moment, for perfection is a mirage that keeps you from the treasures of today. The opportunities before you are ripe for the taking, and your heart knows the way. Trust yourself, take the leap, and let each new experience bring you closer to a life filled with joy, fulfillment, and purpose. Now is the time to live boldly and authentically.

97

Even In the Wake of Tragedy, Life Holds the Promise of Beauty Once More

Though the storm may be fierce and the sorrow profound, there lies within us an incredible resilience—a capacity to heal, to find hope, and to rediscover joy. Through the cracks of our broken hearts, light filters in, illuminating new paths and unexpected blessings. It is in the small moments of kindness, the support of loved ones, and the quiet strength we summon each day that we begin to see the world anew. With time, patience, and courage, the tapestry of life weaves itself into a rich and beautiful mosaic, reminding us that even after the darkest nights, the sun will rise again.

98

Be Patient with Yourself

Have patience with yourself; you are on a remarkable journey of learning, growing, and evolving. Each step, no matter how small, contributes to your development and understanding. Embrace the process, recognizing that growth takes time and often comes with challenges. Be kind to yourself in moments of doubt, and celebrate your progress, however gradual it may seem. Trust that every experience, whether triumphant or difficult, is shaping you into a stronger, wiser, and more compassionate version of yourself. Remember, the evolution of your soul is a continuous journey and you are exactly where you need to be right now.

99

Life

Life is a sacred journey woven with threads of joy, sorrow, love, and growth. Each moment, whether bright or shadowed, holds profound meaning and contributes to the richness of our experience. Embrace the journey with an open heart, cherishing the beauty in everyday wonders and finding strength in the trials that shape our souls. Every step, every breath is a gift, guiding us toward deeper understanding and connection with ourselves and the world around us. Honor this sacred path by living with intention, gratitude, and compassion, knowing that each day brings new opportunities to learn, to love, and to be transformed.

100

You Are Made to Exist In The Frequency of Love

We are made to resonate in the frequency of love, our very essence tuned to its powerful vibration. Love is our natural state, the force that binds us to one another and to the world. It gives us the strength to overcome adversity, the courage to face our fears, and the compassion to heal and uplift those around us.

In moments of struggle, when darkness seems overwhelming, it is love that lights our way, reminding us of our inherent worth and the boundless potential within. By embracing love, we align ourselves with the highest frequency, enabling us to navigate life's challenges with grace and to transform our experiences into a higher understanding.

101

Your Soul Is Saying to You

"The best thing you can do today is enjoy what's here in your life. You have so many blessings right in front of you that are waiting to be enjoyed. A grateful heart attracts more to be grateful for. Anything that is weighing you down isn't yours to carry. Let go and be free. This chapter of your life is the greatest one yet."

Michelle Clare is a multifaceted practitioner with an abundance of spiritual expertise. As a Certified Medium, Angel Intuitive, and Spiritual Coach, she navigates the realms beyond our physical existence. Additionally, Michelle brings her gifts as a Medical Intuitive and Energetic Healer to illuminate the paths of healing and self-discovery. Having survived three Near Death Experiences and having had three Shared Death Experiences—Michelle's journey is marked by resilience and profound transformation. Michelle is excited to share new information about Soul Plans, Shared Death Experiences, and navigating the delicate landscape surrounding suicide.

You can connect with her on Instagram, Facebook, and YouTube by visiting her website at www.michelleclare.net

Printed in Dunstable, United Kingdom